THE FACTS ABOUT
Arthritis

Claire Llewellyn

Thameside Press

Distributed in the United States by
Smart Apple Media
1980 Lookout Drive
North Mankato, MN 56003

Text by Claire Llewellyn
Illustration by Tom Connell

Editor: Russell McLean
Designer: Helen James
Picture researcher: Frances Vargo
Clinical consultant: Frankie Turner, Senior Occupational Therapist,
    Yorkshire Regional Juvenile Arthritis Service, England

Quotes on pages 10 and 21 are taken from *Arthritis Today* magazine.

Splint shown on page 15 supplied by Wristeasy, PO Box 135,
Wetherby, West Yorkshire, LS23 7JJ, England

Thanks to the American Juvenile Arthritis Organization (AJAO) and
National Institute of Arthritis and Musculoskeletal and Skin Diseases
for help with the U.S. edition.

Printed in China

9 8 7 6 5 4 3 2 1

Library of Congress Cataloging-in-Publication Data

Llewellyn, Claire.
    Arthritis / written by Claire Llewellyn.
        p. cm. -- (The facts about ...)
    Includes index.
    ISBN 1-929298-99-4
        1. Arthritis--Juvenile literature. 2. Rheumatoid arthritis in children--Juvenile literature.
    [1. Arthritis. 2. Diseases.] I. Title. II. Facts about (Mankato, Minn.)

    RC933 .L56 2001
    616.7'22--dc21

                                                                            2001027260

Picture acknowledgements: John Birdsall Photography: 5t, 23b. Corbis: Chris Carroll 12;
Jenny Woodcock/ Reflections Photolibrary 26b, 27. Eye Ubiquitous: James Davis Travel
Photography 29; Yiorgos Nikiteas 4t; Paul Seheult 20, 21t; Skjold 10. Sally & Richard
Greenhill: Sally Greenhill 3l, 5b, 22b. Photofusion: Richard Alton 28b; Paul Baldesare
cover background, 4b, 13b; Richard Galloway 9b; Crispin Hughes 24t; Clarissa Leahy 8b;
Brian Mitchell 1, 24b. Rex Features: Vic Thomasson 22t. Robert Harding Picture Library:
8t, 25t; E. Chino 3r, 19t. Science Photo Library: Bill Bachmann 7b; John Banosi cover br,
6t; CC Studio cover bc, 16b; BSIP Edwige 17t; BSIP Leca 18b, 21b; BSIP Taulin 17b; Alain
Dix/Publiphoto Diffusion 7t; John Greim 14b, 18t; Richard Hutchings 26t; Dr. P. Marazzi
15b. Stock Market: Jose Luis Pelaez Inc. 11b; Ariel Skelly 16t; Tom Stewart 28t. Telegraph
Colour Library: Candice Farmer cover bl, 3c, 25b; Chris Ladd 14t; Barbara Peacock 9t;
Martin Riedl 19b; Geoff Tompkinson 13t. David Towersey: 11t, 15t, 23t.

Contents

Words in **bold** are explained
in the glossary on page 30

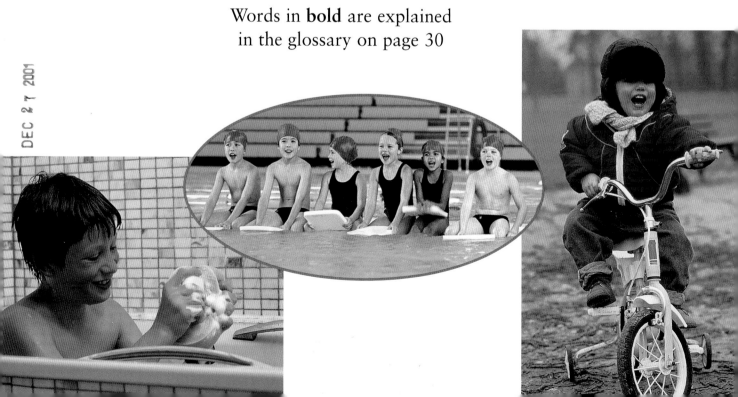

What is arthritis?

Arthritis is a disease which affects the body's **joints**. It makes them feel stiff and painful. We use our joints every time we move, so having arthritis not only hurts, but makes it difficult to get around.

Children with arthritis

Most of us think that only older people have arthritis. This is not true. Many children and young people have a form of arthritis known as **juvenile rheumatoid arthritis** (JRA).

We can bend, twist, and straighten our bodies because our bones fit together at places called joints.

Clues to arthritis

You can't always tell that someone has arthritis, but now and again there are obvious signs. These signs are known as **symptoms**.

Children who have arthritis don't let it stop them having fun.

Arthritis symptoms

- Pain and swelling in the joints.
- Feeling very stiff.
- Difficulty in moving.
- Feeling tired and generally unwell.

This is how some people with arthritis describe their symptoms:

"My knee hurts when I have to stand."

"I feel really stiff when I get up in the morning and when it gets cold."

"I can't move as fast as other people."

"I get tired very quickly."

"I can't keep up with my friends."

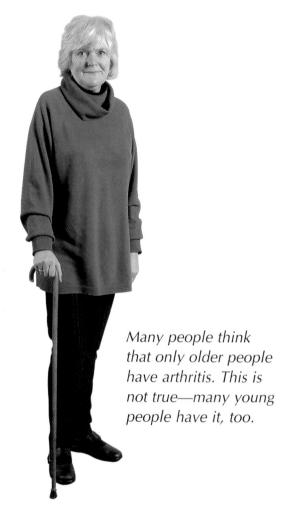

Many people think that only older people have arthritis. This is not true—many young people have it, too.

Living with arthritis

Arthritis can be painful. Some people have mild arthritis, which means there may be times when they cannot run. Others have severe arthritis, which means they are unable to run at all. Arthritis in young people may vary a lot from day to day— and may last for a few months or for many years. "Flares" are when symptoms are worse. "Remissions" are when they are better.

There is often no way of telling just by looking whether someone has juvenile rheumatoid arthritis.

Looking at joints

Joints are places where two bones meet. They have to take a lot of wear and tear. If joints are affected by arthritis, they become painful and may be damaged permanently.

Moving easily

In a joint, smooth **cartilage** covers the ends of the bones. It stops the bones from grinding together and wearing away. An oily liquid called **synovial fluid** coats the joint. This helps it to move smoothly and easily, over and over again.

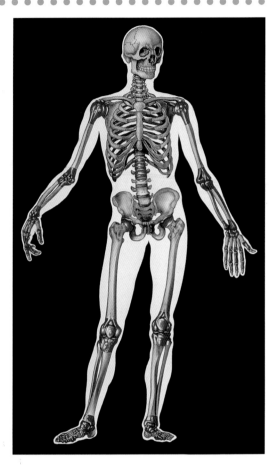

The joints shown in red are the ones most often affected by arthritis.

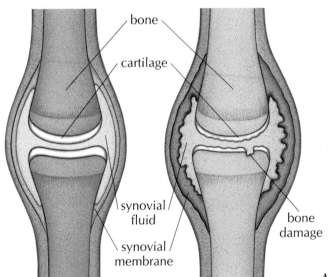

A normal joint

A joint affected by arthritis

Inflamed joints

Joints that are affected by arthritis become **inflamed**. In other words, they are red, tender, and warm to the touch.

A knee joint that is affected by arthritis becomes swollen and painful.

Arthritis can also cause:

- Inflammation in the eyes, which may lead to serious eye disease.
- **Anemia** (fewer red blood cells).
- Tiredness and irritability.
- Loss of appetite and weight.

An inflamed joint, such as this elbow joint, is red, swollen, and stiff.

Thinning cartilage

An inflamed joint makes too much synovial fluid. This builds up around the joint—making it swollen and causing pain and stiffness when the joint is moved. Over a long time, the inflammation can make the layers of cartilage at the ends of the bones grow thinner. Without treatment, this may cause damage to the bones.

Did you know?

- Arthritis comes from the Greek word *arthron*, meaning joint. *Itis* means inflammation.
- Arthritis is a physical condition. It affects the body, not the mind, but it can affect the way you feel.

Preventing damage

Bones are living **tissue** and can heal themselves as they grow. But a joint that has been damaged by inflammation may not be able to do this. Treatment for arthritis aims to calm the inflammation. This makes a person's joints feel less painful and stiff today, and may prevent damage in the future.

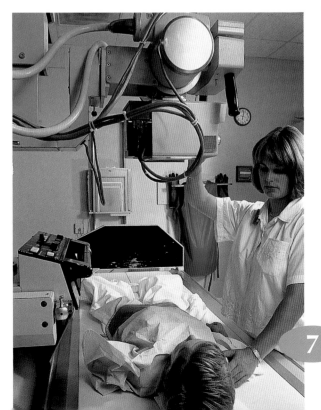

X-rays help doctors to look inside the body and see the condition of a person's joints.

Types of arthritis

Arthritis is a general name that covers a large number of conditions affecting the joints.

Childhood arthritis
Three types of arthritis affect young people in particular—**pauciarticular, polyarticular** and **systemic arthritis**. All three are grouped under the general name of juvenile rheumatoid arthritis.

Pauciarticular arthritis
This affects about half of all children with arthritis. Four or fewer joints are swollen, and sometimes only the knee. The condition can make children feel unwell, but often improves after a few years.

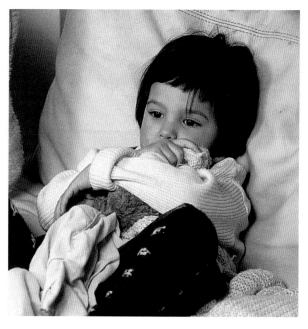

Girls under age eight are most likely to develop pauciarticular arthritis.

Polyarticular arthritis
This affects about 30 percent of children with arthritis. Five or more joints are inflamed, making a child tired and unwilling to move. It often comes on quickly, and spreads from one joint to another. Some children recover within a year, but many have the condition for longer. The longer the arthritis lasts, the more likely there may be damage to the joints.

Polyarticular arthritis is tiring, as it affects many of the body's joints.

Systemic arthritis

This affects 20 percent of children with arthritis. Most are under five years old. It starts with a high temperature and a red, blotchy rash on the arms and legs. At first, these symptoms can be mistaken for an infection. It may be weeks before there is any pain in the joints. Systemic arthritis leaves a child pale, weak, and **vulnerable** to infections.

Systemic arthritis starts with a high temperature. It can last for several years.

Ups and downs

The symptoms of arthritis vary from day to day. Sometimes a child feels well and moves around quite easily. On other days a joint may flare up because of an infection, an injury, or tiredness—but sometimes for no reason at all. The ups and downs of arthritis can be hard to handle.

Looking ahead

It is not easy for doctors to say how a person's arthritis will affect them in the future. It usually depends on how long the arthritis has lasted and how much damage has been done to the joints. Children who have only a few inflamed joints usually make a very good recovery. This is less certain for children whose symptoms return, or whose joints are affected more severely each time the illness flares.

Over half of children with arthritis lose their symptoms as they grow older.

Who has arthritis?

Arthritis can strike at any time, from childhood to old age. It is not an easy condition to adapt to, and each age group faces challenges of its own.

What causes arthritis?

There are many myths about what causes arthritis. The truth is that scientists do not know. There seems to be no single cause, such as climate or diet. Nor is it directly inherited. Doctors suspect that arthritis may be caused by an unusual reaction by the body to an infection.

Juvenile arthritis usually starts in children under the age of five.

Arthritis is *not* caused by:

- Catching cold.
- Getting wet feet.
- Sleeping in a damp bed.
- Eating the wrong foods.
- An injury or fall.

Children with arthritis

Some children develop arthritis when they are very young. This can be a surprise to their parents. If a child is too young to understand the condition, the exercises they need to do to treat the arthritis must be gentle and fun.

"Although sometimes it is very painful, arthritis gets easier as I get older because I can understand what is happening around me."

CLAIRE, AGE 9

When their joints are sore, a teenager with arthritis may need help to dress.

Teenagers

Some children develop arthritis in their teenage years. The change from being healthy to unwell and even disabled can be difficult. Teenagers like to be independent, but arthritis often limits them. The condition means they have to rely on their parents for help, which may make them feel angry and frustrated.

Older people

Different kinds of arthritis affect older people, too. The condition usually begins between the ages of 30 and 50. For many, it brings discomfort, pain, and tiredness. Also, a loss of strength and a weaker grip can make hard work of everyday jobs. The effects of arthritis can be hard to handle, especially for adults who have always been active.

Most types of arthritis affect older people.

Diagnosing arthritis

When children are unwell or in pain, they need to go to the doctor. They may have some tests that help the doctor to identify the condition—in other words, to make a **diagnosis**.

A tricky diagnosis

It can be difficult to diagnose arthritis in very young children. A two-year-old may not complain about a particular joint, but just be generally down in the dumps. Also, swollen joints are much harder to spot on the plump limbs of a toddler. The first signs of arthritis may be when a child limps, tries to avoid walking, or only uses one hand when playing.

Arthritis is difficult to diagnose in very young children, as they cannot describe what they are feeling.

Is it arthritis?

A child who is complaining of pain in a joint or limping may be sent to a **center** at a hospital. There, they see a **pediatrician**—a doctor who specializes in treating children.

The doctor examines the child and asks all sorts of questions. The child has a number of tests, and x-rays may be taken of the affected joints.

Blood tests show up inflammation and anemia, two important symptoms of arthritis.

After the diagnosis

Making a diagnosis is a slow process, and may take several months. This can be a difficult and worrying time. Eventually, after other possible illnesses have been ruled out, a child may be diagnosed with arthritis. The news often comes as a surprise because many people believe that arthritis only affects older people. As they adjust to the diagnosis, both child and parents will have many questions and concerns about the future.

A child who may have arthritis visits a pediatric rheumatologist, who specializes in juvenile arthritis.

Treating arthritis

People who have arthritis are treated in several ways. The treatments help to reduce pain and stiffness, slow down the disease, and prevent long-term damage to the joints.

A three-in-one treatment
Doctors use three different treatments to combat arthritis:
- drugs, which calm inflammation;
- **physiotherapy**, which helps to keep joints moving;
- **occupational therapy**, which helps people with arthritis to tackle everyday jobs.

Children with arthritis may take medicine every day to calm swollen joints.

Drugs
Anti-inflammatory drugs reduce inflammation and relieve pain and stiffness in joints. This allows people with arthritis to use their joints as normally as possible and to exercise more easily. More powerful drugs, called **steroids,** are injected into the joints of people whose arthritis has not improved and whose joints are at risk of long-term damage.

Physiotherapy helps to keep joints moving.

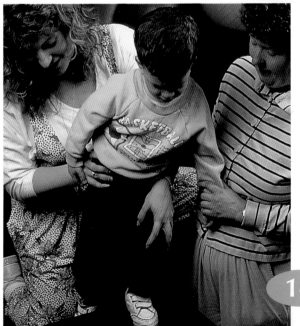

A splint gives support to a weak joint, and helps to lessen pain.

Physiotherapy

Physiotherapy uses exercise to fight the effects of arthritis. People who have inflamed joints often hold them in a bent position. This feels more comfortable, but the joints can become very stiff if they are not straightened or exercised regularly. Physiotherapists work out a program of exercises to keep joints moving as easily as possible, and to strengthen the muscles around them (for more on this, see page 16).

Occupational therapy

Occupational therapists advise people with arthritis about tools and equipment to make life easier. They also make **splints** which keep joints in a good position. There are two types of splint: "working" splints support weak joints, allowing them to be used, while "resting" splints keep joints in the best position when not being used. Splints help to relieve pain, reduce swelling, and prevent damage to joints.

Surgery

Occasionally, a joint becomes so badly affected by arthritis that an operation is needed to replace it. This is a big operation, but it can greatly improve a person's life.

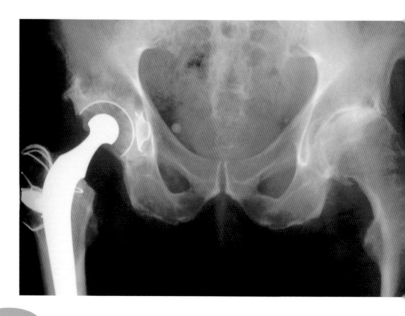

A joint that is badly damaged by arthritis can be replaced. This x-ray shows an artificial hip joint.

Who can help?

People with arthritis may be cared for by a medical team. Each member of the team is an expert in their field, and provides a particular kind of care.

Physiotherapists

Physiotherapists plan a program of exercise, **hydrotherapy** (see page 18), and relaxation to suit the needs of each person with arthritis.

Arthritis often affects the feet. Wearing athletic shoes can be most comfortable.

The physiotherapy program helps to keep an affected joint in a good position, allows the joint to move more easily, and strengthens the muscles around it. Physiotherapists suggest treatments to reduce pain, such as placing a hot-water bottle or an ice pack on a sore joint. They may also advise teachers about gym activities for children with arthritis.

In a physiotherapy session, exercise helps to strengthen muscles, which in turn protects the joints.

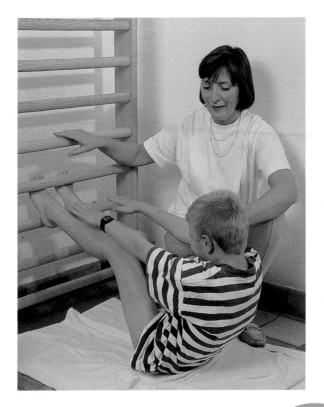

Occupational therapists

Occupational therapists may visit homes and schools to see how children move while taking a bath, playing, writing, or using stairs. They suggest tools to make life easier, such as a padded pen at school or large-handled knives and forks at home (for more on this see page 23). Occupational therapists also make and fit splints, and advise people on looking after their joints.

Podiatrists

Podiatrists are specialists on feet. There are about 35 joints in each foot. Any of these may be affected by arthritis, which can make walking difficult. Podiatrists make special **insoles** to solve this. Insoles hold the feet in a better position.

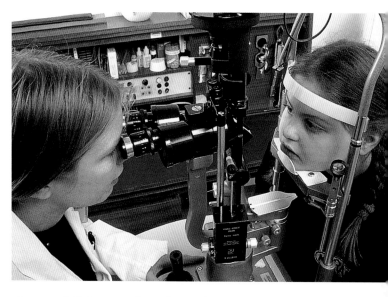

Some children with arthritis have as many as four eye tests a year.

Ophthalmologists

Ophthalmologists test people's eyes for signs of disease. Children with arthritis may develop a particular type of inflammation in the eye. Regular eye tests help to detect the condition so that it can be treated before the eye is damaged.

Support for patients

The American Juvenile Arthritis Organization (AJAO) runs pediatric rheumatology centers around the country. These give information, advice, and support to families which are affected by arthritis.

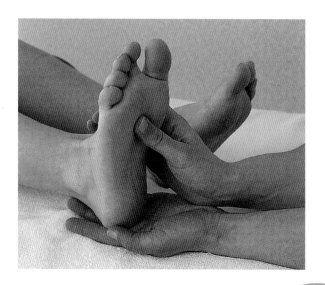

A podiatrist specializes in treating feet.

Exercise for arthritis

Exercise is important for people with arthritis. It keeps joints working, strengthens muscles, and helps to reduce pain. But it takes a lot of time and is very hard work.

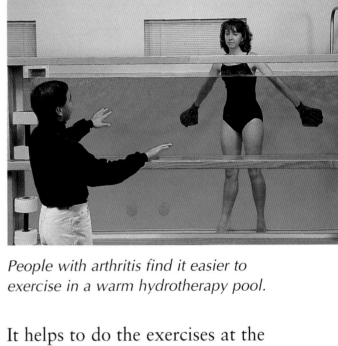

People with arthritis find it easier to exercise in a warm hydrotherapy pool.

Making it fun

A person with arthritis needs to exercise one or two times a day. At times, the sessions can be boring and painful. Having to do them makes children with arthritis feel different from their friends. Parents need to be positive and encouraging.

It helps to do the exercises at the same time every day, perhaps before a favorite TV show. Lively music helps with the rhythm of an exercise, and makes the session more fun.

Hydrotherapy

This is a way of exercising in warm water. The water supports the body, and allows someone with arthritis to move more easily without putting weight on their joints.

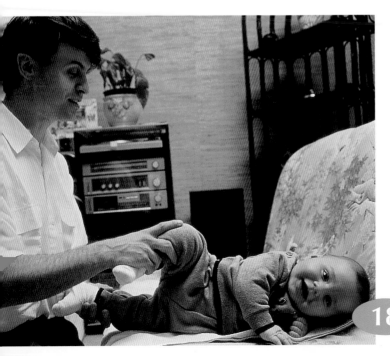

Exercising to music can be more fun for a child with arthritis.

Exercising in a hydrotherapy pool helps to strengthen muscles, while the warmth of the water relaxes the muscles and makes joints less painful. Hydrotherapy is fun, and encourages swimming, which is a great form of exercise for children with arthritis.

Riding a bicycle exercises the joints in the legs.

Swimming is a good way of exercising without putting a strain on the joints.

Other activities

Other kinds of exercise can help children with arthritis. The best kinds, such as cycling and walking, help to keep joints moving without straining them. Teenagers are encouraged to try new sports and stay physically active.

"Some places have the equipment I need and I even went sailing with my teacher. Once I did a sponsored walk on a special flat route."
LEANNE, AGE 13

Visiting a center

Children with arthritis may visit a hospital center. Here, they may have lots of tests and be examined by members of a medical team, including bone specialists (orthopedic surgeons).

First visits
When children are first diagnosed with arthritis, they may visit a center fairly often because they have so many people to see. Later, when treatment is under way, children may visit a center less often—about every three to six months.

What happens at a center?
Firstly, children are weighed and measured to give an overall picture of how well they are. The doctor asks how they have been since the last visit, whether they are stiff in the morning or have any pain in their joints, and how the arthritis is affecting their everyday life.

Visits to a center mean that children with arthritis miss a lot of school. It can be hard for them to catch up on their work.

Then the doctor looks for any inflammation and checks movement in the affected joints. Comparing the results with those taken at the last visit shows if the condition is improving or not.

Testing, testing

Doctors often ask for x-rays or blood tests to check the progress of the disease. X-rays help them to see whether there has been any damage to the bones. Blood tests show up anemia and inflammation, and allow doctors to see how the drugs are working. This helps them to decide whether the amount of medicine a child is taking needs to be changed or not.

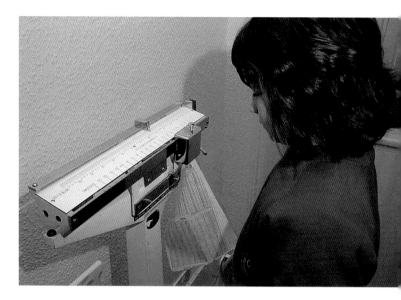

Children are weighed when they arrive at a center.

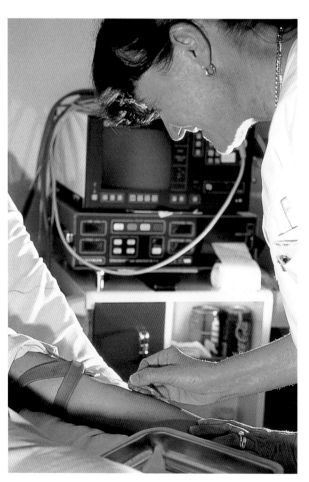

More appointments

After seeing the doctor, a child with arthritis may have appointments with other members of the medical team. The occupational therapist may want to fit a new splint. The podiatrist may need to check a new pair of shoes. The ophthalmologist may need to test the eyes, and perhaps **prescribe** some drops.

"About a year ago we counted that Claire had visited the hospital 81 times—we gave up counting after that."

Mrs. Hill

A nurse taking blood for a blood test.

Family life

Arthritis has a big impact on family life. Caring for a young person with arthritis takes a lot of time and energy. It's not surprising that brothers and sisters can feel a little left out.

Finding the time
For someone with arthritis, the day often starts early in the morning with a hot bath to relieve pain and stiffness in the joints.

A healthy diet helps to strengthen bones and muscles.

Simple tasks, such as dressing, may take much longer than usual. Time has to be found for hospital visits, exercise, and hydrotherapy sessions, too. On top of this, parents may spend a lot of time and energy encouraging a child with arthritis to take their medicines, wear their splints, and exercise every day.

A hot bath in the morning helps to relieve stiff joints.

Diet

People with arthritis do not need to eat a special diet. But they should eat a healthy mixed diet containing **protein** to build up their muscles and **calcium** to strengthen their bones.

Brothers and sisters

Arthritis can affect the other children in a family. Because the disease is so unpredictable, it can cause some last-minute problems. A day out may be cancelled if the child feels unwell. This can be disappointing. Brothers and sisters are usually supportive, but at times they may feel jealous of all the care that a child with arthritis receives.

When a child has arthritis, it affects the whole family.

Special tools, such as this jar opener, make everyday tasks easier.

Changes at home

Occupational therapists often suggest changes to a house to make life easier for people with arthritis—like putting in grab bars by a doorstep and next to the bathtub and toilet. Special tools and equipment help children perform everyday jobs and become more independent.

Helpful equipment

- Cutlery with bigger handles.
- Padded pens.
- Faucet turners.
- Can and jar openers.
- A stool to perch on.
- An electric toothbrush.

Arthritis at school

The hustle and bustle of school life demands many physical skills, and can be a struggle for children with arthritis.

A helping hand

Schools can help a child with arthritis in many ways. The first step is for the parents, teachers, physiotherapist, and occupational therapist to discuss the child's needs. The occupational therapist looks for likely problems, such as writing and using stairs. Ramps, padded pens, or a computer may be the solution. The child's schedule should be planned to avoid long journeys between classes.

A busy school staircase may cause problems for a pupil with arthritis.

Sometimes a child needs extra help for a few hours every week. A classroom assistant may work next to them, helping with tricky physical tasks, such as using scissors. This can help children keep up with their work.

Writing with the help of a computer may be easier than writing with a pen.

24

Children with arthritis may need more time to change clothes than other children.

Schools may need to:

- Let children with arthritis play inside with a friend at break.
- Provide a helper.
- Give them hooks and lockers on the end of a row.
- Allow them to wear specially comfortable shoes.
- Allow them to leave class early to avoid the rush, giving them more time to get around.

Exercise

A physiotherapist can advise schools on exercise. Swimming is very good for children with arthritis. Other sports, such as soccer or football, may be ruled out when symptoms flare.

Missed lessons

Some children with arthritis miss a lot of school. As well as visiting a center, they may need to stay in the hospital sometimes, for injections or check-ups. Children who miss school can feel left out and it helps if classmates keep in touch. But most children who have arthritis enjoy school life and do well in their work.

Educating others

School staff need to be sensitive to the feelings of children with arthritis. No child wants to stand out from the crowd. Teaching other pupils about arthritis helps a great deal, too. Not knowing about the condition can lead to teasing and even bullying.

Swimming is good for children with arthritis. They can compete equally with others.

Living with arthritis

Living with arthritis is not easy. The condition can prevent people from being independent and doing things that others enjoy. It's important that they have plenty of support.

Being independent

All children learn to become independent as an important part of growing up. Most young children can wash and dress themselves from the age of about five, but this may not be possible before age ten for a child with serious arthritis—perhaps because their joints are just too stiff.

Learning to dress yourself is an important step on the way to independence.

Sometimes a person with arthritis may need to walk with crutches, but this is rare.

Young people with arthritis need to practice everyday tasks, such as doing-up buttons, turning door knobs, going to the toilet, and managing stairs. Parents need to avoid being overprotective and should help their children to help themselves, even though this may take some extra time.

Negative attitudes

Many young people find it hard to tell other people that they have arthritis because of the myth that it only affects older people. A few are bullied and teased by children who don't understand what arthritis is.

Being positive

Young people who are picked on for having arthritis may feel that life has handed them a raw deal. They may have low expectations of what they can achieve. But those who are given support enjoy a more positive attitude.

Special breaks

A normal home and school life is important for children with arthritis, but a weekend away with others who have the same condition can be a real boost. In some places, weekends are run for teenagers with arthritis. They provide a break from home, help with making new friends, and give a taste of activities not tried before. The trips help young people to become more confident and realize that they're not alone.

Children with arthritis can try out activities such as canoeing on a weekend break.

Questions people ask

My joints are very sore.
Will exercise damage them?
Exercises do not cause damage.
A physiotherapist can advise on
the best exercises to do and how
often to do them. In the long run,
exercise reduces pain, inflammation,
and stiffness—and helps joints to
move more easily. It also makes
muscles stronger. Swimming is one
of the best exercises, and the effect
is best when the water is heated.

*Joints in the hand are often affected by
arthritis. It's important to exercise them.*

*A lap-top computer can help a child
who has problems holding a pen.*

My hands are so stiff that
I find it hard to keep up
at school. What can I do?
Handwriting is a problem for many
people with arthritis. Some teachers
give out photocopied notes so that
a child with arthritis doesn't have
to make notes of their own. Padded
or chunky pens can help, as can a
lap-top computer for children who
know how to type. This cuts down
on handwriting and can make a
difference to a child's schoolwork.

Do warmer climates help arthritis?
People all over the world have arthritis. A warm climate does not affect the disease itself or prevent it progressing, but the weather can affect some people's symptoms. Some find that warm weather is better than cold. But for others, cold crisp days are the best of all.

Will I be able to drive with arthritis?
Most adults with arthritis are able to drive, but it depends on how severe their arthritis is. Adjustable seats and power steering are helpful. An automatic car helps, because the driver does not have to shift gear.

Warm, sunny weather is good for some people with arthritis. It helps to reduce swelling and stiffness in their joints.

Are splints really necessary?
Yes. The aim of a splint is to make sure a joint stays in the right position so that when the arthritis burns itself out, as it may do, there is little damage to the bones. When a joint is uncomfortable, children often try too hard to protect it and stop it from moving as it should. Splints help to correct this.

Glossary

anemia A condition where there are not enough red cells in the blood. Someone with anemia feels tired and weak, and looks pale.

anti-inflammatory Designed to reduce swelling and redness in a part of the body.

calcium A chalky white material that is found in bones and which helps to make them hard. Foods such as milk, cheese, and yogurt contain a lot of calcium.

cartilage The smooth, slightly soft and springy material that cushions most of our joints. Cartilage also forms the bendy parts of our skeletons, such as the ridge of the nose.

center A place where doctors and nurses treat a range of diseases or conditions.

diagnosis Discovering what type of disease a person has.

hydrotherapy A type of exercise in warm water that helps stiff joints to move more easily and strengthens muscles.

inflamed Sore, red, and swollen.

insole A special lining inside a shoe or boot, sometimes made with extra support or cushioning.

joint A place in the body where two bones meet.

juvenile rheumatoid arthritis A general name for the types of arthritis that affect young people. JRA may affect bone development and a child's growth.

occupational therapy A type of treatment that helps people to solve physical problems caused by a condition such as arthritis.

ophthalmologist An eye expert.

pauciarticular arthritis A type of juvenile arthritis that affects four or fewer joints.

pediatrician A doctor who specializes in treating children.

physiotherapy A type of treatment that uses exercise to treat someone who has had an accident, an illness, or an operation.

podiatrist A specialist doctor who treats the feet.

polyarticular arthritis A type of juvenile arthritis that affects five or more joints.

prescribe To order a certain drug or medicine for a patient.

protein A nutrient that the body needs to build new cells and repair itself. Meat, fish, and milk contain lots of protein.

splint A device that helps to support a weak or painful joint.

steroids Drugs used to reduce severe inflammation.

symptom One of the signs of a disease. Stiff, inflamed joints may be symptoms of arthritis.

synovial fluid The oily liquid that coats a joint and allows the bones to move smoothly and easily.

systemic arthritis A type of juvenile arthritis where the child has a high temperature and sometimes a rash, and feels generally unwell.

tissue A group of cells that work together to do a particular job in the body. Muscles and organs are made-up of tissue.

vulnerable Open to attack.

x-ray A special photograph that shows some hard substances inside your body, such as bones and teeth.

Useful organizations

Here are some organizations you can contact for more information about arthritis:

American Juvenile Arthritis
    Organization (AJAO)
1330 West Peachtree Street
Atlanta, GA 30309

Tel: 404/872-7100
    800/283-7800
Website: www.arthritis.org

National Institute of Arthritis and
    Musculoskeletal and Skin Diseases
    Information Clearing House
National Institute of Health
1 AMS Circle
Bethesda, MD 20892-3675

Tel: 301/495-4484
Website: www.nih.gov/niams

Kids on the Block Inc.
9385-C Gerwig Lane
Columbia, MD 21046

Tel: 410/290-9095
    800/368-KIDS (5437)
(An educational program using puppets to show the effects of JRA.)

Index